Keeper of Secrets

Oct 2011
For Eve,
I share the
same story. B

Bonnie

Keeper of Secrets

Bonnie Lis Norris
&
John Norris

iUniverse, Inc.
New York   Bloomington

Keeper of Secrets

iUniverse books may be ordered through booksellers or by contacting:

iUniverse
1663 Liberty Drive
Bloomington, IN 47403
www.iuniverse.com
1-800-Authors (1-800-288-4677)

ISBN: 978-1-4401-8111-5 (sc)
ISBN: 978-1-4401-8110-8 (ebook)

Printed in the United States of America

iUniverse rev. date: 10/20/2009

Contents

To Joanne

Acknowledgments

I want to acknowledge several people who have been critical to my survival during my journey. To JLB, I love you. To my dear friend, BN 2nd, sharing our parallel lives has meant the world to me. To CDM friends for the many teachings and the encouragement I received.

I would like to thank my family and friends. They were very important in this process. Even the littlest thing, such as making pancakes for breakfast before heading to the airport, provided much comfort and joy to my soul.

I am grateful to Dr. Keith Grieneeks for his professional insights as well as his support and encouragement to follow my dreams with this book. Special thanks to my editors at Verve Editing.

The rest of my family and friends want their names to be private and so I honor their wishes.

Author's Note

This book is based on my memory of events that occurred long ago. I kept diaries at the time but they are long lost. I have reconstructed what happened to the best of my ability and by questioning family members. I have changed the names of some individuals to protect their privacy.

Introduction

The jetliner was several hours from its destination at Detroit Metro Airport. The whole flight would take a little more than four hours, a testament to the distance I had traveled from the town in which I grew up to my current home in the Pacific Northwest. After twenty years in Seattle, I no longer thought of my arrival in Detroit as "coming home." I was a Seattleite through and through, proud to be from a progressive city in a beautiful corner of the nation. Still, I was looking forward to visiting my family, especially my older sister Donna, and attending my twenty-fifth high-school reunion.

In the seat next to me, my fifteen-year-old daughter, Mandy, was sound asleep and oblivious to the rest of the world. I pushed my seat back, no doubt to the dismay of the passenger behind me, wrapped the thin airline blanket tightly around my shoulders, and closed my eyes. As I tried to nestle into the narrow seat, I was again confronted by the question I'd been repeating to myself for weeks: Should I tell Donna?

I had kept a secret from my family, and most especially from Donna, for more than thirty years. Donna had recently separated from Ray, the man she'd married when she was a senior in high school. But she couldn't make up her mind about whether or not to sign the divorce papers. Should I tell her? I'd kept my secret all this time because I didn't want to break up her marriage and ruin our relationship. But now … I wasn't so sure that remaining quiet would be best for either of us. In my half-asleep state, I began composing a letter to Donna:

Dear Sister, I need to tell you something about Ray, something you need to know while you're making your difficult decision ...

The flight attendant roused me from my thoughts with offers of soft drinks and pretzels. Any diversion from the monotony of this long flight was welcome. I dropped my tray and asked for a diet soda.

On the one hand, I thought that Donna deserved to know what had happened, especially at a time when she was making a critical decision regarding her marriage. On the other hand, I had all my old standby reasons for keeping my silence: Wouldn't I be intruding in her life? What if she didn't believe me? What if she reacted by never speaking to me again? Who knows how someone will react to such an explosive revelation.

Watching the bubbles cling to the sides of my plastic cup, then rise and pop, rise and pop, I finally decided to say nothing during my stay. After all, I had a class reunion to enjoy and Mandy was getting to visit her grandmother and other relatives. Why risk spoiling all of that? It was a lot safer to just keep my silence.

Mandy and I arrived in Detroit and rented a car. We drove to my mom's house in the suburb of Dearborn, the heart of Henry Ford territory. Dropping my luggage in my old room, I flung myself on the bed, drifting into a daydream as old memories of childhood and high school came flooding back. I still loved the comfort and security of that room. My experience in high school had been the typical mix of great times and agonizing embarrassments, and I was nervous as I anticipated seeing my classmates for the first time in many years.

Once Mandy and her grandma were settled, I dressed myself for a night on the town with my old pals, Debbie and Sue. We planned to go to dinner, then head to the class reunion icebreaker event. Debbie and Sue were fellow Thunderbirds, classmates from Edsel Ford High School, named for Henry Ford's son and the former president of Ford Motor Company. The corporate headquarters is just down the road from the school. Henry Ford's stamp was all over our neighborhood, and many of our parents had been company employees. I had kept in touch with Debbie and Sue all these years even though they married and stayed in the Detroit area, while I had moved away to a life out West.

Eagerly I sat at the restaurant table with Debbie and Sue; they had the scoop on many classmates who lived in the area. We giggled throughout dinner as we ran through a list of expected attendees. We talked about the crushes we'd had in high school, and I pointed out with interest that Jack, my first boyfriend and first love, was on the list.

Jack and I had started dating our sophomore year and remained together for five years. But I hadn't seen him since I moved to Seattle, right after I graduated from college, eighteen years earlier. Obviously, seeing him again would be the most interesting event of the weekend. What old feelings and emotions will surface, I wondered. Will we have a chance to talk in private and rehash old times? What will he look like? Bald and overweight? Slim and dashing? Will he have had a successful career and a good life? Will he recognize me? Will I recognize him?

After dinner, we headed to the bar that was hosting the icebreaker. Why was I so nervous? This is silly, I scolded myself. For heaven's sakes, I'm happily married. And yet, butterflies swirled in my stomach as if I were still that sophomore going on my first date. I let my friends enter first while I followed along, half hiding behind them, taking in the crowd. We stood there for a few moments, feeling awkward and self-conscious, noticing groups with half-familiar faces but afraid to catch anyone's eye and not recognize someone we should.

"Hey, there's Teresa!" I exclaimed, feeling the relief of spotting a good friend from the past. We walked over to her group and began reintroductions amid exclamations of surprise and pleasure as we recalled friends from long ago. Then, out of the blue, Teresa grabbed my arm and said, "Bonnie, this is Jack."

My body stopped as I stared at the man standing beside her. "Bonnie, this is *Jack*," she repeated. I just stood there, frozen like a popsicle. All I could feel were my eyes moving back to Jack and then to Teresa as I tried to comprehend who he was. It finally sunk in when I recognized the twinkle in his eyes. "You're Jack!" I blurted.

"Um, y-yes," he said, with a tentative smile. "How are you, Bonnie?"

With complete spontaneity, I wrapped my arms around him and squeezed. I was immediately at ease, perhaps because I could tell how apprehensive he had been at seeing me after all this time. Jack looked good, still youthful and healthy. That twinkle in his eyes was still there too, along with his wonderful smile. I wasn't surprised to hear that he had four kids; he had told me many times he wanted a large family. Jack and I chatted, but with all the other classmates playing "Hey! Aren't you …?" we didn't get a chance to spend time together and really talk. By the end of the night, my girlfriends and I had had a wonderful time, and we were eagerly looking forward to the next night's main reunion event. As I left the bar, I was sorry that I didn't get that much time with Jack. Maybe tomorrow, I hoped.

More than two hundred alumni, roughly half our graduating class, showed up for the main reunion event. We all wore the name tags that twenty-five long years had rendered essential. I would have walked right past many of my former classmates had I passed them on the street. A few were recognizable when they broke into a still-familiar grin or when I heard their voices. But I relied on name tags a lot.

Once again, my friends and I were too busy meeting and chatting with our classmates for Jack and me to get much of a chance to talk. When the night was over, I walked to my car and saw him heading on foot to his parents' house. I offered to give him a ride. At first he declined, perhaps thinking of the impropriety of two married, former lovers being alone in a car together, far from their spouses. But I insisted. "Come on," I said. "Of course, I'll give you a ride."

Once he got into the car, we were finally able to speak freely and privately. By the time I pulled into his driveway, we found ourselves deep in a serious discussion of our past relationship. To my surprise, Jack was apologetic. He felt that he had treated me badly in high school. At first, though, he kept his thoughts about it superficial. "Remember the time I threw you in the pool at my uncle's party?" he asked. "I always felt bad about that because I knew you didn't want to be thrown in."

"Well, we were young," I said, thinking that kind of behavior back then a pretty minor offense. I doubted that was the real reason he felt guilty. I prodded him a bit more and finally he revealed what was really bothering him. He said he felt that he had pushed me too hard to have sex with him back then. But I had never felt that, and I told him so. He looked at me now, the doubt plainly in his eyes.

My main regret, I explained to Jack, was that I just couldn't lighten up and relax at that age. Hell, twenty-five years later I often was still more uptight than I wanted to be. "Remember, Jack, that you told me I looked like a stone? I was never able to just relax and enjoy our relationship."

"Well, it didn't help that I was always trying to be sexual with you," he said. Jack explained that, in retrospect, he felt he had probably been too pushy with intimacy at too early of an age and was afraid that it had harmed my later life.

It was so difficult to encapsulate my entire story in a few sentences, to explain why I was who I was in high school. But there was one overarching reason for my cool behavior, and now that we were sharing concerns about our past, I felt the need to share my secret with him.

I went for it. "Do you want to know why I had a shield around myself all that time? Why I was so unable to loosen up?" I asked Jack. "Well, I was sexually molested by a family member. I haven't even told my brothers and sisters yet. And I couldn't even begin to tell my mother."

I was on a roll, but I brought the conversation back to us, to his concern. "You see, it wasn't you," I said. "You and I were just having a normal teenage relationship; well, as normal as it could be, considering. I was carrying around so much baggage in those days. I was a sensitive person to begin with. That's why I was often so uptight. But believe me, my relationship with you was a relief from all of that. It was me, not you." There, I had done it—I had started the process of admitting what had happened to me to my friends and family back home.

Jack looked at me calmly and with compassion. He was silent, but I think he believed me, and my explanation lifted a bit of the guilt from him. I felt a tear slide down my cheek. "Don't worry," I told him. "I'm okay now, because I've been through a lot of soul searching, and I've worked to make myself sound and whole. I was ashamed of myself for a long time, but I'm not anymore." As I wiped the tear away, I realized that I felt good about our conversation. I felt relieved that for the first time I had told my greatest secret to someone other than my spouse. I wasn't sobbing or screaming, and the world wasn't ending. I simply described what had happened—a simple disclosure, a few simple tears, and a weight off my soul.

Jack didn't make a display of his emotions; he just told me how sorry he was that it had happened to me. But I knew that he felt better about our past relationship after our talk. Maybe some things even made sense to him now. We said good-night, and I headed the car toward my mom's home.

That night I lay in my childhood bed and closed my eyes. My mind wandered as I drifted into sleep. *Dear Sister, I have something to tell you. I don't know where to begin ...* I practiced in my head as I nestled into the pillow and let sleep carry me away.

Part 1
My Youth

Chapter 1:

The Neighborhood

Like most of the families in the Polish Catholic neighborhood of Dearborn, mine had lots of kids. Nine, in fact, and we weren't even the largest household in the neighborhood. Four of the kids were my brothers, two were my sisters, and two more were cousins who came to live with us after my aunt died in an auto accident. In age order, we were: Karen, Donna, James, Brad, Dave (cousin), Joe, Bonnie (me), Joanne (cousin), and Tommy. I was number seven.

Boys, boys, boys! Growing up with a pack of highly active sports-minded boys, I was introduced to the competitive side of life at an early age. The competition was by no means limited to the playing fields. After long afternoons of playing our exhausting neighborhood kid games, there I would be, starving, elbow-to-elbow with my even more ravenous brothers, heaping our plates with mounds of mashed potatoes, meat, and vegetables. It wasn't until high school that I discovered most girls didn't routinely wolf down three hot dogs at a time for lunch. We'd gobble down our food, then race back outside into our great outdoor kid zone until the light faded.

The neighborhood was devoutly middle class, influenced by both the Vatican and the American work ethic, which meant large families with little loose money to spend. My dad—around five feet ten, stocky, and extremely athletic—was the eldest son of an alcoholic father and had dropped out of school at a young age to go to work. English was his second language. His parents had immigrated from Poland, lived in Pole Town Detroit, and never learned the English language. In those days, everyone in the neighborhood spoke Polish, so what was the need? Hence, Polish foods and traditions were part of my dad's life and the lives of his kids as well. After serving in World War II in Patton's Third Army, Dad returned to his job at the Ford plant, to which he devoted forty-six years. On the side, he played, coached, and refereed baseball, basketball, and football.

My mom was also part of the working class, of English and German descent. Her family had roots in the South; years earlier, her ancestors had traveled to Detroit in search of jobs. She loved Southern food but learned to cook Polish foods to please her husband. My mom stood about five feet five; she was brunette and skinny. She loved watching sports, which made for a great partnership with my dad, who was always playing on a sports team. The two of them produced a lot of tall, skinny, athletic children.

My mom was immensely proud that she had put herself through college and became a registered nurse. While she quit for a while to start our family, she went back to nursing when she was done having babies and Tommy and I were in elementary school.

We lived in a pretty rowdy neighborhood in those days, with plenty of opportunities for my brothers to get into trouble. I was too shy and cautious to get involved in their escapades myself, but I enjoyed quietly watching in the background as they found various and novel ways to bring the wrath of the adult world down upon them. Fortunately, their brand of trouble was relatively harmless, and they usually avoided involvement with neighborhood gangs or attracting the attention of the law.

One typical summer began with my cousin/brother Dave occupying the doghouse. Just before school let out in June, we were having lunch in the elementary school cafeteria. Dave told us that he could kick the shoe off his foot into a big garbage bin across the room. My brothers argued for a while about whether he could actually perform this prodigious feat of athleticism. With his reputation now publicly at stake in the crowded lunchroom, Dave took aim at the garbage bin, stepped forward, and launched his hard-soled shoe with a mighty kick. The shoe sailed past the garbage bins, smashed through the picture window behind them, and landed on the grass beyond. We all immediately doubled over with laughter.

"Oh, my God, Dave's in trouble," my brother Joe yelped, pounding his hand on the table with glee. We doubled up with laughter again as the lunchroom attendant ran over and nabbed Dave. Another day, another trip to the principal's office for one of the boys. Dave's only solace was the knowledge that he wouldn't be in the doghouse long. Surely one of my other brothers would soon find a way to replace him.

Dad's method of discipline was to have the boys assume a three-point football stance while he administered a fairly vigorous swat on their behinds. Alternatively, he'd escort the guilty party down to the baseball field and make him pick up glass, an activity that was followed by an exhausting workout of running after ground balls, fly balls, and pop-ups.

My mother's mode of discipline was altogether different. So was her temperament; her moods would swing wildly. It took almost nothing to set her into a wild rage—an off-hand comment or what she considered an improper reply to a question. Then all hell would break loose. We learned to be non-responsive to her questions. In one of the kitchen drawers, she kept a certain wooden spoon. When angered, she'd whip it out and apply it to our backsides, wild-eyed, lost in fury. We'd run the minute she had it in her hand. If we were quick enough, we'd be out the kitchen door, around the house, and safely down the sidewalk before she could get close. If not, we'd end up with smarting welts on our butts or backs.

All the kids developed techniques for coping with Mother's moods. I turned both to sports and my sister Donna for comfort. I was a natural athlete, and team sports were a perfect match for me. Growing up with so many brothers, I had spent my childhood playing baseball and basketball. Best of all, sports are oriented toward physical action rather than talking. It was a relief to me just to have to take coaching directions, which was easy as I'd been on the receiving end of my dad's coaching since I'd been able to walk. Sports became an essential escape for me and a way to assert myself in an entirely simple, action-oriented way.

Sports were my physical outlet, but Donna was my emotional safe harbor. She was blonde, tall, slim, and very smart. Of my two older sisters, Donna often was given the task of babysitting my baby brother, Tommy, and me. Karen seemed much older and to be doing her own thing. Oh, I'm sure Karen had plenty of household chores and babysitting tasks. I just don't remember. There was ten-year gap in age between Karen and me, just large enough to put us on different paths.

Later on Karen and I would become quite close, but at that point in my life, it was Donna who was tender, gentle, and understanding toward us younger kids. Donna was my emotional rock. When I was small, I would crawl into her bed in the early morning hours and savor hugs and cuddles with her. Our relationship was more than just a simple sisterly one; she became my stand-in mother figure and my source for guidance when I needed it. We even shared the same birth date. For years, I cherished having both of our names on one cake on our special day.

As the number of kids increased, it became obvious that we were outgrowing the house, so during my elementary years my parents added square footage by expanding the upstairs area. The large bedroom upstairs was part of the new construction. For years, my siblings and I would argue about who deserved to live in the "large bedroom upstairs." During the first part of my youth, the girls held rank over the boys. The four girls shared the large bedroom, which was big enough to hold four single beds, dressers, and night stands, with enough room to walk around.

The two eldest, Karen and Donna, had half of the bedroom for their twin beds, while Joanne and I, the two youngest, shared a double bed on the other side of the room. Karen and Donna put fear into Joanne and me to never, never go to their side of the room. They even hung beading from the ceiling to the floor to divide the room in half. Of course, I wondered what the mystery was on their side of the room. Fear worked well on me, however, so instead Joanne and I stayed on our side, fighting over the blankets at night, trying to stay warm. Joanne wasn't as athletic as I was so we didn't hang around together much outside the house.

Near the end of my grade-school years, a series of rapid, drastic changes shifted the family dynamics. Karen went off to college. Then, after many years of living with us, Joanne and Dave moved out. Their dad had remarried and wanted his kids to live with him again. Donna began dating a guy named Ray, a high-school classmate of hers. Ray was talkative and stout, with short, dark hair and thick glasses.

During their date nights, Ray would come over and wait in the living room while Donna finished getting ready. Tommy and I seized the opportunity to hang out with him. We would casually appear in the living room and, inevitably, he'd start horsing around with us. He'd jokingly tease us and rub our heads; it was fun. We loved the attention. Ray showed up, and Tommy and I would have some fun. In my eyes, Ray looked like such a cool guy.

Donna and Ray got married late in their senior year of high school. Donna was pregnant; Ray became my first brother-in-law. A few months afterward, the baby was born, a boy named Jason. Ray and Donna rented an apartment two miles away. That left just four boys and me in the household. I was delighted because I finally had my own bedroom and my own bed. At last I had space for myself and my thoughts. It meant that I had to move out of the large bedroom and into the small bedroom at the end of the hallway, but I didn't care. I was thrilled; this bedroom was all mine, upstairs and away from the majority of people. I was happy with the move.

However, I soon began receiving a concentrated dose of unwanted attention from Mother, who was now in menopause. I was already at her emotional beck and call; it had always been easier for the boys to ignore her or walk out the door when she lost control. She may also have realized that my painful shyness made me an easy target and outlet for her own pain.

There were things I liked doing with my mom. Working again as a nurse and with fewer kids in the house, she had more cash available for things like sewing material for our clothes. She and I would go to the local fabric store and enjoy an afternoon of picking out material to our hearts' content. We'd have a splendid time during the car ride home talking about the fabric and all the possible outfits we could sew. But magical times with my mom seemed to have a twist to them. When we arrived home, my mother told me to go inside the house and check on my dad's whereabouts while she waited in the car. I'd run into the house, check on my dad, and run back to the car. "He's in the backyard," I'd report or offer some other location.

"Good, now go in the house and sneak the package of material into the sewing area without your dad seeing you, and don't tell him about this," she'd say.

I did what my mother told me to do. I'd sneak the material into the house and return to the car to tell her that the coast was clear and she could come inside. Instead of it being a fun secret between "us girls," the Mother-orchestrated sneaking around was a dangerous game that would have dire consequences if Dad found out. I would be nervous all day, wondering if Dad was going to ask me about our shopping trip. At the time, I wasn't mature enough to realize that Dad rarely engaged in Mother's paranoia and wouldn't have questioned her about buying material for clothes. Thus, what should have been a lovely time with my mother was twisted into something sinister and secretive. At an early age, I learned to behave as though nothing was wrong while hiding secrets from my dad. Even worse, I was hiding my anxiety from the world. No one could know the inner turmoil in my stomach by looking at my face.

With Mom seemingly incapable of showing tenderness and empathy and Dad unable to physically and emotionally express his love, there were no loving arms wrapped around me and no soothing of my emotions when I needed reassurance. I was taught simply to keep my mouth shut and obey authority. I often wondered was this style of raising kids invented by my parents or the way the majority of children in our area were being raised?

Mom also paid for my sewing and gymnastics lessons, and she would often drive me to and from the gym. These took care of some of my basic needs, but what I really longed for were the glimpses of affection she occasionally showed me. Simply being around her as we took care of normal tasks was a source of some comfort as long as I didn't upset her. In fact, my brothers later made pointed comments about how lucky I was to be given so much more than they had. They weren't there to see what else I had been "given."

Chapter 2:

Drive the Car

"Bonnie, the phone's for you," Mom yelled up the stairwell.

It was Donna. Was I available to babysit? Wow, my first time as a babysitter, I thought, and I'd make fifty cents an hour. To my twelve-year-old mind, that was major bucks. Imagine. Fifty cents an hour for playing with my nephew. Jason was now a toddler, and Ray and my sister had bought a home within bike-riding distance from my house. "Sure!" I readily agreed. "When will you pick me up?"

The first few times I babysat, Donna and Ray remained close by at a neighbor's house, playing cards, and were only gone for a few hours. They'd come home, and Ray would drive me home. Someone in the house was always up when I returned, and I'd run into the living room, yell a quick "Hi!" from the staircase and beat feet up to my room. Eventually Donna became more comfortable leaving Jason in my care, and they would come home later in the night. I'd usually fall asleep on the couch until they woke me up by knocking at the door.

I'd bounce off the couch quickly and head to the front door, then raise my body up onto my tippy toes while using my hands to balance myself. The wood door had only one window, several inches above my height. I moved the curtains just enough to peek out, making sure it was Donna and Ray before I unlocked the door and let them in. For some reason, they didn't use their own house key; instead they waited until I unlocked the door. Maybe it was because they did not want to sneak up on me.

Ray teased me in his joking way about being so timid, as if throwing open the door in the middle of the night would have been a better thing to do. I wasn't sure what to make of his jokes. But I knew that there was a fun way to tease people, and there was a not-so-fun way. Ray's teasing often worked both ways. Usually light and playful, he would occasionally drift into an edgy, judgmental mode that seemed to be designed to make his target feel small and demeaned. But I dismissed this side of his teasing because he was one of the more interesting people in our family circle. He had a gift for telling stories and jokes, and he spoke in a disarmingly frank and down-to-earth manner that naturally drew listeners into whatever he was saying. He'd have been a great politician.

To a young and naïve girl, he sounded like he knew everything. He voiced strong opinions on a range of subjects, in a manner that usually was so personable and laced with good-natured humor, it was difficult to object to anything he said. In any case, our family had not been brought up in an atmosphere that encouraged back-and-forth, challenging conversation. Dad was quiet, and Mom was too unpredictable. To me, Ray seemed to embody what it meant to be a grown-up: smart, informed, confident. I thought Donna had made a great catch. Ray was a mature and knowledgeable husband who went to work every day, provided for his family, and seemingly had life by the tail. Certainly, I was in no position to question what he said. And I didn't really want to.

At first, when Ray drove me home after a night's babysitting, we didn't talk. We didn't even have the background sound of a radio. There was just silence. He stopped his car in front of the house, dropped me off, and into the house I'd run. So it surprised me one night when, a few blocks away from my sister's house, he asked if I wanted to steer the car. Sure, I nodded, thinking, How cool! Finally I get to drive a car! I slid over close to him, climbed on his lap, and happily took the wheel. His invitation was exciting in my very innocent mind.

I placed my hands on the steering wheel, concentrating on the road and keeping the speeding car between the white lines. Fun!
Then it happened.

I gasp as my body involuntary twists. It's a gesture that is ignored by him.
Ray whispers in my ear, "Look, you don't want both of us to die, do you?"
I shake my head no. I speak not a word.
"If you let go of the steering wheel, we'll both die!
"Don't let go of the wheel!
"You don't want us to die, do you?" he quietly says in my ear.
I shrug my shoulders.
My body tightens as Ray starts to unzip my pants. In my mind, I gasp a little louder, but I am soft-spoken, probably no one heard. Ray whispers over and over, "Now, watch where you're driving."
Suddenly, he begins petting me.
I've never been touched like this before.
I heard about this, but is it really happening?
I know this is wrong, and yet I can't move.
I don't understand why my body doesn't move or scream or cry.
I am still. I am motionless.
He can't be doing something wrong, I think; this must be okay.
But I know it's not.
He wouldn't do this; he is family. I am so confused.
My eye sees only the road.
I concentrate on steering the car so we don't die.
I block everything else out.
No thoughts are allowed.
Quietly we drive the few miles to my parents' house.
Ray continues; I dutifully steer the car.

How slowly time seems to pass.
Finally, we are a few blocks from my house.
Ray zips up my pants and tells me, "The driving part
is over. You'd better get back to your seat."
I do as I'm told. I am a robot.
He never says a word about not telling anyone.
Neither do I.

When we reached my house, I jumped out of the car and walked inside. My parents were waiting up. I didn't say a word to them; I just went upstairs to bed. I went to sleep in a daze. Did that really happen, I asked myself.

The next morning, life continued as though nothing out of the ordinary had happened. I went downstairs to eat breakfast, and everything seemed the same. I ate the same hot oatmeal, sat in my usual seat at the table. Maybe nothing had changed. I always had been a quiet child, but now I felt as though I was living in a quiet world with chaos all around me.

It wouldn't last long, my desire to stay in my quiet internal world—not in my busy household. I soon learned that I would have to do something to challenge my shyness. I was in the upstairs hallway, which was next to my bedroom. My clothes closet was located there, and I considered the area to be part of my bedroom. It was my territory. I decorated the hallway in the same blue-and-white color scheme as my bedroom. It was my sanctuary in a house full of people.

So when Joe approached me in *my* hallway, I knew something was up. He told me that I had to go to the store and pick something up for my mother. "Why me?" I asked with a guarded stance, ready at any moment to block a punch. Ever since I could remember, my two brothers, Joe and Tommy, would punch each other at the slightest provocation. All siblings fight, right? Well, that was definitely true during my childhood. Usually one of my brothers cocked his arm, then in came the swing, with a punch landing on my shoulder. I, in turn, would make a fist and, as hard as I could, plant a mean punch on his back between the shoulder blades. Then I'd run away very fast. My two brothers never ganged up on me; it was always a fair one-on-one fight. None of us ever won a fight, and there wasn't any bloodshed, only invisible marks that our parents never would see. On this day, however, there was no punch from Joe.

"She told *you* to go to the store," I said.

"No, you have to do this," he replied.

"Why?"

"Because she needs Kotex, and I'm not about to go into a store and ask for Kotex." My jaw dropped. All I knew about Kotex was that it was personal and embarrassing and vaguely dirty. Why should *I* do this, I thought, annoyed. But I was a girl, and this was a "girl" product, and the next thing I knew, I was on my bicycle riding the half mile to the drugstore. I purposely chose a little corner neighborhood shop so I wouldn't be recognized. Heaven forbid that someone I knew saw me purchasing the mysterious Kotex. I waited and waited outside the store until it was empty of customers.

"Hi, I need to buy Kotex," I said to the clerk, dying inside because, of course, he was a young man.

"Sure, what kind?"

Oh, he's going to drag this out forever, I thought. He's going to ask what size, what color box I want, what's it for ... Before you know it, the whole neighborhood will be trooping in to help me out with this purchase of Kotex.

I pointed to the box I wanted, hoping that I'd picked the right one. I was a bundle of nerves and prayed for the clerk to hurry up. I paid and finally, *finally*, the shameful box was safely out of sight in a plain brown paper bag. I rode my bicycle home as fast as I could and hurriedly found Joe, giving him the bag and the change. Whew, I thought to myself. Made it! Several months later, the same thing happened. It became a routine; my brother would get me to run this errand for him. It seemed like I was spending most of my adolescence buying Kotex for my mother. Why couldn't she just buy it herself? Every Saturday, she and I would go grocery shopping. Why couldn't she buy the Kotex then? But there was absolutely no way I could have talked to Mother about it. She would have emotionally blackmailed me by announcing at dinner in her high, harsh, whining voice that "Bonnie wouldn't buy something so simple as Kotex. Can you image that, after all the things I do for her?"

Before long I had another babysitting assignment from Donna and Ray. I didn't even hesitate. When the time arrived for Ray to drive me home, Donna thanked me and I, dutifully and void of all emotions, got into the car. My body was frozen. I sat there, still as could be. I tried to be invisible. I was hardly breathing. Ray drove in silence. And … nothing happened.

Maybe the other night was a one-time episode, I thought, as we neared my house. Maybe he'd just had too much to drink? I wasn't sure. Ray didn't say a word the whole drive home. I jumped out of the car, feeling a thousand pounds lift from my shoulders. Things are back to normal, I thought. Thank God!

The following weekend brought another babysitting job, but this time Ray encouraged me to "drive" the car home. To this day, I don't know why I trusted him. The next thing I remember, I was steering, and he began feeling between my legs. This time, however, I felt something that was foreign to me.

Ray's hand seems different this time. I don't know what it is.
Ray begins to whisper in my ear, "You know you like it. You want it, don't you?" Want what, I wonder.
Ray has plunged several fingers into my vagina.
I am numb.
"Now watch the road," he cautions.
I'm thinking, we can't both die because of me.
I'm looking at the road, scared and confused.
Ray keeps telling me that I like it.
Is he right?

The worst of it is that I can't stop my body from reacting.
I hate myself. I'm evil for feeling these thrilling, new sensations.
Ray kisses my neck, and I break out in goose bumps.
I am disgusting.
I am more confused.
I desperately want to get home safe.
I tune out Ray; the robot version of me reappears.
Suddenly, we are close to my house.
How did that happen? I am back in my head.
Ray removes his hands and zips my pants back up.
He tells me to move off his lap and get back to my seat.
I do what I'm told; after all, I am an obedient and good girl.
We stop in front of the house; I hop out of the car.
Once inside, I wave to my parents.
As I head upstairs to my bedroom, I mumble a good-night.
I don't cry or think.
I get my PJs on and head straight into bed.
I fall sound asleep.

There were many rides home, and many incidents like this. It got less scary, and that made it even more confusing. I was helpless in response to his command that I "drive"; I went into automatic pilot and never said no. I didn't think consciously about it; I just did as I was told. It shouldn't be surprising that I didn't say no; after all, I was a kid and not skilled in decision making. To me, adults meant authority, submission, agreement, and compliance.

When it happened, it was like a roller coaster. My body was being turned on sexually while my insides were terrified, and I was left in jitters afterward. Before I knew it, the ride was over, and we were in front of my house. As always, I'd run into the house, go up to my bedroom, and go to sleep. This became a routine.

I babysat almost every weekend, but these incidents happened at random. Sometimes he'd leave me alone, sometimes not. I did as I was told, period. Mentioning it to Mom was unthinkable. I had no idea what her reaction would be, but I knew she would handle it in the most embarrassing way possible. Most important, I wouldn't have dreamed of ruining Donna's life. So I kept quiet.

Chapter 3:

I Want to Be Special

A memory:

I am playing outside. Something upsets my young mind.

I can't control or explain why or even how this happens.

I begin running from the house.

I have no control over my body.

I begin sprinting as fast as possible, running to nowhere and to no one.

"There she goes again," I hear one of my brothers say.

"She's trying to run away—again!" another says.

Same run, just a different day. I do this randomly over a period of a year.

"Let's get her."

I turn my head and look behind me.

Here come my brothers, chasing after me, like a posse.

Sometimes I run barefoot in the snow. It doesn't matter what the season is ...

I have no feeling when I'm running. I just run and run and run.

My breathing grows more labored.

I look again, and the gap between me and my brothers has closed.

I'm not fast enough.
Finally, one of them grabs me. I stop running and
surrender to his hold on me.
I turn and follow them back home, guarded by the
posse .
I am doomed; there is no way out.
"She's home," one of my brothers announces to my
parents as we walk into the house.
I drag myself up to my room.
My only sanctuary.
Alone there with my worn-out body and emotions, I
lie down on the bed.
No one comes and talks to me.
The clock ticks slowly.
No one comes at all.
Crying is only for real people.
I do not cry.
I am a prisoner; the posse lives in the same house.
Without thought, I get myself ready for bed; it matters
not what time of day.
In bed, I softly close my eyes.
Whew, I am exhausted.
I am blank inside.
I wish for nothing.
Wishes are only for real people.
I am not real.

Donna held many of the family birthday parties and barbecues
at her house, so I was frequently there during big gatherings.
Often after dinner, Ray would be in his homemade workshop
in the back of the house where he worked on his special projects.
At every chance, I'd make a beeline to join him and help. There,
amid the clutter of his tools and parts, he and I talked while he
worked on his projects. Just the two of us.

"Come, hold this board while I put the glue on," Ray would say. "Now, hold the board one *pubic* hair away." I'd giggle at these kinds of comments, feeling embarrassed but also sort of grown-up. I spent many a time in Ray's workshop, listening to him drop sexually explicit words as though it were perfectly normal. I knew they were forbidden words, and I knew it was wrong, but his magical ways didn't stop me from giggling at their sound.

Usually, after an hour or so, someone would call my name, saying that it was time to leave. I'd dash into the house, grab my stuff and be ready to go, wondering if others had heard the sexually explicit words. I'd look around and guess that nothing was wrong because everyone always acted the same as before.

◆   ◆   ◆

In the seventh grade, our teacher encouraged us to write journals. It would help us sort out difficult things going on in our lives, she promised. I made my own diary and began describing my frustrations with my mom. The teacher said that keeping a diary could be a great release for us, and I found that to be true. However, I didn't dare write about Ray.

During the quiet of the evening, I'd write down my feelings, inarticulate but raw and honest. Then I'd stuff the book under my mattress. One day after walking home from school I walked into my room and caught my breath. My stomach fell through the floor. There was my journal, lying on top of my bed. I would never have left it out like that. Mom must have found it and read it, I thought. Shaking, I reviewed what I had written, trying to read it through her eyes, hoping against hope that it didn't sound as bad as I was afraid it did. But it was all there, from my descriptions of her emotional manipulation to my reactions to her terrifying rages. Worst of all I had written the word "BITCH" in bold letters to describe her. That was the page that faced me as I looked at my bed. Anxiety shot through my body like an electric bolt.

I spent the rest of the day in my room, deathly afraid to go downstairs, dreading dinner time. Would she fly into a rage in front of everyone? Did I hurt her feelings? To my surprise, she did nothing. I ate my usual heaping dinner. In those days, I could be an emotional wreck, but I never lost my appetite. It was eerily quiet at the dinner table. Everyone knew something was up, but true to our training, no one said anything. We all kept our eyes on our own plates and ate our dinner. Once again the master of psychological warfare had employed an inventive and effective strategy. By not mentioning the diary, while at the same time ensuring that I knew that she knew, she kept me off balance.

That evening I took the diary and hid it well in my bedroom; unfortunately, however, fear won, and I stopped writing in it. I was too afraid that Mother would find and read it again. Nevertheless, the need to let my feelings out was overwhelming, now more than ever. I was in such a circle of torment. I couldn't talk to anyone about the frustration and anger boiling inside me. I sat and stared out the window, numb. The next thing I knew, I had shredded a sock that was lying beside me. Thus began something of a ritual for me. Instead of writing in my diary, I would tear up one of my socks and then throw the shreds of material away. Luckily I was able to hide my new habit better than I did writing in my diary; the clothes dryer got blamed for a lot of missing socks.

Air conditioning was not yet common in our neighborhood, and throughout the summer all the windows in the house were usually open to catch a breeze. One day in the summer during my junior high school years, over the hum of the fan in my upstairs window, I heard the loud voices of my parents downstairs, arguing. "Here we go again," I thought.

Fights between them were common, but this one quickly became louder and nastier than usual. I walked out of my bedroom to the top of the stairs, making sure I couldn't be seen. Then I overheard something that stunned me: my mother telling Dad that he had to choose between her and me—the "me" being *me*, the kid listening at the top of the stairs.

Her or me? Could I have heard right? Choose what? Why? What was she talking about?

Suddenly the door slammed as Mom stormed out of the house. I ran to the window in time to see her stuffing her suitcase into the trunk of the car, then get in and drive away. A silence filled the house. I went back to my room, wondering what in the world was going on. She was making Dad "choose" between her and me?

I wanted so badly to telephone and ask Donna what was going on, but I couldn't get up the nerve. Asking my brothers was out of the question. They'd not have any more of a clue than I did and, anyway, they weren't around that day. The entire family was programmed not to speak about such personal and emotional subjects. We never did. We didn't even know how.

Eventually, I walked down the stairs to the living room, looking for Dad. I spotted him through the window, painting the outside of the garage just as he had been doing before the fight started. Earlier in the day, I had been painting with my dad and was taking a break when the fight broke out. I decided to rejoin him.

Dad loved to paint, and I think it was a kind of therapy for him. Sometimes he'd be out in the garage after dinner, just painting boards for no reason but to be painting. First one color, then another. Maybe that was an escape from the world. I picked up a brush and started applying paint to the garage, not saying anything except hello. Dad didn't mention the fight. I don't think he knew how. He lacked the experience, the education, and the other skills necessary to discuss something as complicated and sensitive as this with any of his kids. Maybe he realized this, and so he kept quiet rather than making things worse by stumbling around, trying to explain something for which he had no words. I just kept painting.

After several hours, I'd had enough, and I spent the rest of the afternoon in my bedroom, on pins and needles wondering what was going to happen next. Finally, at dinner time I wandered into the kitchen, where Dad was making hot dogs for dinner. I joined him for a silent dinner.

I spent the following morning helping Dad paint the garage and, again, we barely said a word. This was actually pretty common with Dad, since he spoke so little even in the best of times. He was great at teaching someone how to field a groundball but had no skill for small talk. Just before noon, I went up to my bedroom to get ready for lunch. One of my mother's friends, Betty, stopped by to try to reconcile Mom and Dad. I scooted to the top of the stairs so I could overhear the conversation. I heard Betty telling Dad that Mom would only come back home if I apologized to her. "Apologize for what?" I thought to myself. I didn't understand this situation. The stalemate continued the next day, and Dad stayed home from work, which was highly unusual. This time, Mother came to talk with Dad directly and, again, she said that one of the things she wanted was an apology from me.

Mother must somehow believe I'm a rival for Dad's love, I thought. That's what I heard, listening from the top of the stairs. I had no idea how to process something like this. Alone in my room with my thoughts, I knew that I hadn't done anything wrong. But I also knew that I wanted to please my mom; I wanted her to be happy and to feel loved. I wrote a letter of apology and left it on her dresser. It took another day for Dad to find it and have it delivered to my mother, who moved right back in soon afterward. Nothing was said to me, and we all returned to our daily routines as though nothing had happened. It was our typical response to a situation that desperately needed discussion.

Now, I doubt the fight between my dad and mom was really about me. Mom was desperately insecure and became jealous whenever she had any reason to feel slighted. Perhaps when she saw me painting with Dad, she felt that he should be spending time with her instead. But to think that they found a letter from me on their dresser—offering an apology for something I did not even entirely understand—and never discussed or even acknowledged it to me amazes me to this day.

Dad had not made any effort before or after that crisis to create special dad-and-daughter time. Today, people recognize that, even in large families, kids need to be the sole focus of their parents' love and attention from time to time—maybe especially in large families. But it just wasn't done back then and definitely not in my family.

Dad had a hard time making his feelings known. When he did talk, which was pretty rare, it was usually about the Detroit Lions or the Tigers, or about the local neighborhood teams he coached. Like many in his generation, he was uncomfortable displaying emotions or discussing his feelings. He demonstrated his love for us in his own understated, patient way. A lot of our interactions with him were on the ball fields, where he would show us the finer points of playing our positions. In many circumstances, that would have been enough for us kids. But in a house where the mother was not psychologically fit to give us the love we needed, it left a hole in our hearts.

My mom worked the day shift at the hospital. Dad worked the evening shift at Ford, so he was often at work or asleep when I was at home. The balance of his free time usually was occupied with coaching or playing baseball and basketball. It seems that there is a fine line in a household when a daughter needs daddy attention and the wife needs husband attention. Both want to be the special one. Many times, my mom seemed to be missing her husband, wanting him to comfort and tell her life would be okay. I wanted the same thing.

In a bizarre and twisted way, Ray filled my need for male attention. At least, *he* talked to me. With his funny stories and one-way conversations, I found myself craving time with Ray inside his workshop.

Chapter 4:

Pendulum

To my great good fortune, the effects of Title IX—the law that broadened high-school and collegiate sports programs to include females—were just being felt as I entered high school. I was able to participate in coed gym classes, which were much more fun than the girls-only classes. I also enjoyed the benefit of having had a childhood that consisted of extensive training in the fine arts of fielding ground balls and swooshing jump shots from Dad and my brothers. Thus, even as a freshman, I found myself in the starting lineup of several varsity sports teams. The success I found on high-school playing fields was wonderful for my self-esteem, and all the exercise was an essential release for the weighty tensions I experienced at home.

Around this time, Donna and Ray bought land about a forty-five-minute car ride from my parents' house. They and my nephew lived in an RV while they built their new home. With several bedrooms, kitchen, and a bathroom, the RV seemed huge to me. Parked on their land, the RV stood in the location of their future home, alone on ten acres of land. Donna and Ray had moved to the country to build their dream house.

Gone were the days when I could conveniently ride my bike over to their house. This meant I was no longer their babysitter and, thus, Ray wasn't able to get me alone for months. During this time, two significant changes occurred in me. First, I no longer had the desire to hang around Ray; instead, I behaved like a puppy around my sister Donna. I now craved *her* attention and time. Second, my frozen inner self began to thaw.

♦   ♦   ♦

"Nice catch," said my girlfriend, Casey. "Yep," I replied, "I have good eye and hand coordination." Casey shouted, "Gee, Bonnie actually talks." I smiled back. "Well, don't tell the world know; you're embarrassing me." As I walked around the party, a beer in my hand, I was thrilled to be looking at the hot guys. "Isn't this cool to be here?" I asked Casey. She said, "Let's go to the bathroom to check our makeup." We always went to the bathroom at least once during a party, to check our makeup and hair. "Okay, Casey, I'll follow you."

Thus began my attraction to high-school social parties and drinking beer. I was a typical teenager; the more I drank, the louder my voice became, and my barriers began melting away. However, because I was an active athlete, I was strict about not becoming drunk; instead, I drank enough to feel good. I really liked beer, and I really liked feeling good. It was a welcome relief from all the anxieties and self-doubt I was experiencing.

When I wasn't spending my weekends partying, I dedicated myself to finding a ride out to Donna's place. My heart sank because I wasn't yet sixteen and thus was unable to drive to the country. My mind worked to find a solution because they lived just far enough away that I would need a car to visit. And then a solution revealed itself.

Typically, on a Friday night someone in my household would drive me to where Ray worked and drop me off so I could meet him at the end of his shift. Ray's work was a family-owned business that built office interiors. Many of Ray's cousins and even some of my family members worked there. It had a huge warehouse with adjacent offices. At the end of his shift, Ray, looking physically worn out and sweating, would drive me home. His workplace was about thirty minutes from where their new house was being built. The thought was that Ray's work place was the halfway point between their new place and our house. Since someone in my family usually went on Sunday to either help with the construction or visit Donna and my nephew Jason, I would get a ride home with that person. It was a convenient plan: Friday get a ride with Ray, spend the weekend at the house with Donna, and on Sunday get a ride home with someone. Since I wasn't the babysitter, Ray wouldn't "bother" me, I believed. Hey, I thought, finally life is going to be better. An illusion.

One particular day stands out in my memory. After being dropped off at Ray's workplace, I went into the office. There were a number of other employees in the area, which gave me some feeling of security. Ray said that he wanted to take me on a tour of the enormous warehouse next to the offices. I wrinkled my nose, not wanting to be alone in a big warehouse with him. One of the other employees in the office said, "Yeah, haven't you seen it yet?" Another added, "Ahh, go on, it's great to see." It was hard to say no, so I nodded my head yes.

Ray took me along the path to the warehouse, describing some of the buildings in detail. I didn't pay attention to his description; I was just happy to see other employees as we walked. Soon we came to a flight of stairs leading to the second floor.

"Come on upstairs," says Ray, "I want to show you something."

I shake my head. No.

"Oh, come on, I'm not going to hurt you," he teases.

Again, I shake my head.

"You're chicken, aren't you?" he laughs.

Later, I'd ignore such juvenile prompting, but as a juvenile, I am unable to just slough it off.

I shrug my shoulders ambivalently.

My voice is still frozen.

"Oh, come on," he presses.

I continue to just stand still.

My thoughts are in disarray, my body is in shock, but I manage to shake my head. No.
"It really is worth seeing," Ray says.
Childish credulity and years of "obey-the-adults" conditioning overwhelm my caution. I step forward and follow him up the stairs, then down one of the aisles.

I was nervous, like Goldilocks entering the forest. I no longer even heard him as he prattled on about the treasures of the warehouse. I just walked closely behind him. As I looked up, there were large stacks of industrial supplies. My, my, the forest is thick and intimidating, I thought. I wished that I didn't feel so scared.

The next thing I know, my body is jolted
He turns and presses me against a wall.
I didn't see it coming.
I'm trying to figure out what is happening to me, unable to speak.
This is the first time he has been so physically aggressive toward me.
He is trying to get his hands inside my pants.
He is winning as my body tightens up from fear.
Frozen and stiff.
But something has changed inside of me
My body begins to resist him.
I wiggle to get out of the physical hold he has on me.
It is no use; I feel like a trapped animal, not a human being.
I know that I am defeated.
I'm a pet dog that is being forced to obey its master.
And now he wants to do disgusting things to me.
I can't shout because I'm too embarrassed.
Then, my luck turns before his hands actually get inside my pants.

We hear another employee coming to that part of
the warehouse.
He lets go of me.
Quickly, we take a few steps away from each other
Relief washes over me.

We walked back to the employee lounge. I was stiff inside and
wanted to be invisible. I felt embarrassed and ashamed. I stood
in the lounge and wondered who, if anyone, saw us. I didn't say
anything, but then I never did around strangers or, hell, anyone.
I thought to myself, surely someone here saw this. Then it struck
me: Good heavens, he's at his work, acting like this. He's being
incredibly reckless or egotistical, or both.

When we arrived at his house that night, we greeted Donna
as if nothing at all had happened. It was such a feeling of safety
to see her. She was my security blanket but didn't even begin to
suspect why. I knew I was safe around Donna. The night passed
uneventfully. We ate dinner; then Donna and I watched TV while
Ray worked in his new shop.

◆   ◆   ◆

One weekend I stayed over an extra night since there was no
school on Monday. Hey for me, I thought; more Donna time.
That Sunday night, after the rest of the family and our friends
who had been visiting that weekend left, I heard a shout from
Ray, calling for Donna and me to come help him. We stepped
outside the RV, noticing darkening skies and the wind picking
up. It looked like it would storm. Donna and Ray were building
a one-level, three-bedroom ranch-style house with a basement.
The house's framed walls were up and standing, but they needed
reinforcement. Donna, with Jason watching her, took one side and
held up a large two-by-four to shore up the frame. I dutifully went
to the opposite side of the house and held up a similar board. My
arms were stretched up over my head, holding the board, when
Ray came over to nail it in place.

Suddenly, I can feel him groping me from behind.
My shock is total.
Donna and their son are only yards away.
This can't be happening, I think.
It takes a minute to sink in.
A slight glance with my head.
He has laid down the hammer and nails and now has his hands on my body. Once again my programming and juvenile decision-making faculties betray me.
"Hang on to the board. You don't want the framing to collapse," he says.
I hang onto the board. I do.
My focus is on the board. Focus, Bonnie, on the board.
I become aware; I cannot block out what he is doing.
Damn my melting walls of protection!
He does what he wants with my body; I still don't say a word.
I am terrified that Donna will see.
I feel like scum.
How could I do this again?
How could I let myself be manipulated into a compromising position when he is around?
To my surprise, it is over quickly, but the ugliness remains.
He didn't wash his hands before he groped me.
I feel gross and dirty and powerless.
I don't want to feel, I don't want to feel, I don't want to feel.
I can't help it, I feel worthless.

Then as if nothing had happened, Ray picked up the hammer and nails and reinforced the framework as I held the board. Then he high-tailed it to the other side of the house where his wife and son were standing and nailed in the boards there. There he was, working next to his family, his fingers still moist from me. My stomach lurched.

Afterward, we all retreated to the RV and bedded down for the night. When I was by myself, I wondered if my sister had seen what happened. This was the first time he'd molested me while she was nearby. But the next day Donna drove me home and mentioned nothing. When I got home, I felt empty and disgusted and disgusting. And I had no one to talk to. I felt so alone and filled with self-loathing. I needed an escape from my reality. It wasn't a party weekend, so beer was out of the question. I had given up ripping and shredding socks. I didn't feel like jogging. Walking around the house, I soon found an escape. It was not as healthy as my earlier outlets, ripping apart socks or exercising. In fact it was the opposite of healthy: candy, specifically, chocolate, and lots of it. My mom was a candy eater herself so there were always bags of it in the house.

Mom kept her bags of candy in the kitchen closet, up high on the top self. Her stock was rarely depleted. Taking a bag of chocolate from my mom's stash, I quickly returned to my bedroom. In wild need for relief, I tore open the bag and began feeding my face, bite after bite, with chocolate. It only took a moment for the chocolate to smooth and ease my body into paradise. Out of control, stuffing my bloated stomach, it was hard to stop. I was now in heaven. I had a mild ache in my stomach, but I didn't care. I convinced myself that the ache was from chocolate and nothing else.

Soon, I began hiding bags of chocolates in my room and diving into them when life's struggles became too intense. Oh, how the comforting feeling of a sugar rush soothed my surging emotions. I'd overindulge in candy until my stomach hurt. Then I would torture myself with remorse, thinking how shameful it was to be so weak, what a terrible person I really was, how fat and ugly I'd become. I could feel my clothes tightening around my hips and waist. Usually the next day, I would work out twice as hard to punish myself for my binge. I'd promise myself to change my destructive ways, but my resolve would rarely carry me through my next emotional trauma.

Fortunately, my fix of choice never developed into drugs, but I can understand how they would be attractive to kids with emotional challenges. One moment in my life, I'm a successful student and athlete with lots of attention and friends; I'm normal. Then the pendulum swings, and I'm being molested.

I ate a lot of candy that week and had occasional thoughts of not wanting to live. Shame washed over me. I felt like less than dirt under a rock. I looked in the mirror. Man, I'm ugly, I thought.

Chapter 5:

She Is a Pawn and Doesn't Know It

At the end of that summer, the house finally was finished. Donna was so excited. At long last, she could move out of that cramped RV. I wanted to see the place and share in her excitement. I called, and we made the usual arrangements for me to get there. I oohed and ahhed at the brand new home, happy for my sister.

The weekend started off great. Donna and I shared time together, with me helping on her current decorating project. Soon afterward, Donna had to take the car into town on an errand with her son. She asked me to go with her. For some odd reason, I just shook my head no, not able to get any words out. So I didn't go with her, and she left me alone in the house. Ray was outside in his workshop. After a while, he came inside.

"Hey, Bon, do you know what a blow job is?" he asked.

"No," I said, and shook my head. Oh, God, what's coming next, I wondered.

Ray laughed at me. "How could you not know what a blow job is at your age?" After a few minutes of teasing, he went back to his shop. Wow, I thought, no touching, no pressure. That's it? What gives? Relief flooded through my body. A short while later my sister returned; I was safe again. I enjoyed a good night's sleep in the brand new house. Maybe it would mean a new beginning.

I woke up the next morning, and my first thought was: Hurray! It's Sunday, and I'm at Donna's! Donna always made pancakes and bacon for breakfast on Sundays. To me, she was the best cook in the world. Her pancakes came with a heaping stack of loving energy. I craved her love and ate her pancakes until I was stuffed. It was like falling into a sea of love.

Afterward, she and I moved to the living room to digest our breakfast while her son played outside. We sat so she could keep an eye on Jason through the sliding glass doors in the room. Normally, we would do arts and crafts or I'd help her with some sewing or whatever project she was working on at the time. But that day we just sat. Out of the blue, Donna turned to me. "Ray tells me you don't know what a blow job is," she said. "Is that right?"

I wanted to disappear. I was embarrassed and humiliated. All I could do was nod my head. Yes.

"Well, let me tell you what it is."

I sat there and listened to Donna educate me. I was silent through the ordeal. I didn't dare tell her that in fact I really did know what a "BJ" was, but I hadn't answered Ray's question because I thought, I'm a kid! And the whole thing seems perverted and weird and totally foreign and it makes me embarrassed. Even talking with Donna about it is embarrassing. But I couldn't say any of that. I remained quiet while I listened to Donna explain the procedure using clinical language, like we were in a health class.

What Donna didn't explain was what in the hell Ray was doing asking her little sister such questions, and why in the world this didn't set off all kinds of alarm bells in her mind. Later I thought, why did Donna decide that Ray's revelation meant I needed to be educated, and not that Ray was a pervert? I was too young to think like that then, however. I just listened to Donna explain and then nodded my head, showing that I understood. I was just glad when the conversation was over.

For the rest of the day, I felt odd being around her. There would always be this issue between us: I no longer felt 100-percent safe and secure around Donna. Ray had ruined that. In a roundabout way, Donna didn't realize that Ray was using her.

Later at dinner when I looked at a Ray, my stomach began to tighten. He knew that I had learned what a blow job was from my sister—his wife. Fear and anxiety made me shiver inside but didn't stop me from eating a large amount of dinner and dessert. Second helpings, please.

◆　　　◆　　　◆

My mom had a favorite saying, derived from some old folklore: "New house, new baby." Being from a large extended family, I must have heard her use that phrase a hundred times. So it came as no surprise to me when, soon after Ray and Donna moved into their new home, she announced that she was pregnant with her second child. "What did I tell you?" crowed Mom. "New house, new baby."

I was fascinated to be around Donna and her swollen stomach, yet my weekend visits to her house became less frequent; high-school sports and friends diverted my attention. I was getting older and beginning to take a keen interest in the boys at school, so I no longer felt the desire to cling to my sister quite so closely. Instead, my visits to Donna's house became more of a group activity with Mom, Dad, my younger brother Tommy, and me trooping over regularly to see the progress of the pregnancy. Ray was usually in his workshop (which I had stopped going to), so I had no alone contact with him. It was a peaceful and happy time for me. We'd enjoy a good meal and then an evening of riotous card games. And there was always the underlying excitement of a new baby on the way.

The family was extra excited that the baby was due around the same time as Donna's and my shared October birthday. We were hoping that all three of us would be born on the same day. How cool would that be?

But a few days before our birthday, Donna went into labor. Shortly afterward, she delivered a baby girl, named Wendy, just two days before our day. Darn it!, I thought. But Donna had wanted a girl very much, and now her dream had come true.

While Donna rested, Ray spent most of the time at the hospital or at work, so I was detailed to babysit my nephew. I ended up staying over a couple of nights at the house, in the guest room that was now the new baby's room. Excitement and baby energy was everywhere in the air. A sense of comfort had taken over my being. I wasn't even scared to be there with Ray and Jason without Donna. After all, Donna just had a baby, so nothing would happen, right?

As night fell one evening, I was comfortably cozy, lying in bed, admiring the way Donna had decorated the baby's room. It had been a good day babysitting my nephew. He's a fun kid, I thought to myself. I drifted off, tired and happy.

Suddenly, I'm shocked awake by a warm, wet feeling in my ear.

Oh, no, Ray is here, and he has his tongue in my ear.

All I can think is how gross it is and how trapped I am, once again.

My body constricts and fear runs through my veins. I am fully awake now.

Ray whispers in my ear, "Let me put it inside you." I shake my head no.

His hands are now caressing me, massaging between my legs.

"You know you want me," he says.

I'm terrified. No! This can't be happening

I had thought the abuse was over, but this is the worst episode ever.

I want to cry, scream, or both. But I am silent.

"You'll be okay, I promise that I won't come inside you."

I lay still.

He continues his whispering and stroking, on and on, repeating himself.

Suddenly, Ray's tone of voice changes.

He is starting to get angry.

I don't understand; Ray has always whispered in a mellow, intimate voice.

As his tone becomes more and more harsh, I get more and more scared.

My heart is pumping furiously; it feels like it will jump out of my body.

I want him off of me, but I can't say a word.

There's no one else in the house except my young nephew, asleep in his bed.

The thought that I'm alone with this monster overwhelms me.

Ray switches back to his whispering and smoothing voice.

"Come on Bon, I'll withdraw just in time."

The guy thinks I'm worried about getting pregnant!

Doesn't he have a clue that I'm terrified out of my wits? Can't he see how perverted and wrong his actions are?

My thoughts race through my head.

He is family, the husband of the sister I idolize, the sister who is in the hospital with a brand-new infant daughter, and here we are.

I'm quiet for a moment.

Oh, no! Ray assumes that I am about to say yes, just to make it end.

He is quiet, and his mouth remains within an inch of the side of my face.

Nibbling on my neck.

This moment of letting down my guard is difficult.

I am torn by his power over me; it feels like I'm under a spell.

Without conscious warning, I finally shake my head no again.

I don't know where that defiance to his command comes from.

I continue to shake my head: No, no, no .Back and forth.
Then, just like that, it's over.
Ray stands up and leaves without saying a word.
He stops short of "doing it."
My body is left lying on the bed. Moist, stimulated.
I straighten out the blankets and wrap them around me tightly, like I'm in a cocoon.
I feel strange—sick with embarrassment and guilt, afraid of anyone finding out.

My life lessons up to that point had all had the same conclusion: saying no to an adult meant punishment later. I knew that Ray would find a way to ridicule and tease me in front of others until I felt worthless. But that night I didn't even care. I curled up in a tight ball and, thankfully, fell back asleep.

The next morning, Ray made breakfast. We were sitting at the table: Ray, my little nephew, and me. Ray served us scrambled eggs. When we were finished eating, Ray turned to his son and said "I thought you didn't like eggs."

My nephew looked thoughtful for a moment. "Oh, yeah," he said, and promptly threw up his eggs. Ray shouted angrily and cleaned up the mess. Ha! I thought to myself, that's what I should have done last night.

The entire family paid many visits to Donna's house over the next few months; everyone wanted to see the new baby. Ray didn't touch me after Donna returned from the hospital; in fact, to my memory, Ray never molested me again. And something odd began to happen to me. My body seemed to come up with its own solution to the Ray problem. I'd show up at his house, and I'd immediately come down with diarrhea. I'd end up either lying on the couch or sitting on the toilet during nearly every visit. I'd try to be as inconspicuous as possible, but Mom began to notice that I was in the bathroom an awful lot.

"My God, what is wrong with you?" she asked. "Every time we get to Donna's house you get an upset stomach. What on earth is wrong?" "It's the well water," I said meekly. And she seemed to believe me. Everyone did.

Chapter 6:

Ugly Thighs

I looked at myself in the mirror as I got myself ready for my date. I was a junior in high school who hated herself from the waist down. Oh, why do I have to have such ugly thighs? I thought to myself. I loved the look of a ballerina, and there I was, shaped like an offensive lineman.

I promise I'll go on a diet tomorrow, I told myself. Turning away from the mirror, I picked out my clothes carefully and then shoved some candy in my mouth. I wanted to show some of my feminine side but at the same time retain some modesty. After all, I didn't want to look like a slut. I'd been dating Jack for several weeks, and I wanted it to continue. I liked him, and it was fun to have a boyfriend who would take me out on dates that I could later discuss with my girlfriends. It was all so new to me and so exciting.

Running down the stairs, I saw that my older brothers were home. Oh, great, I thought to myself. Wonder what they'll do tonight? They were having fun locking the front door and teasing me that they weren't going to let my boyfriend inside until he passed their test. "Better yet," one of them suggested, "Let's lock the door and turn all the lights out and act like no one is home!" I smiled and made my way to the entrance, unlocked the door, and stood guard, waiting for Jack. Moments later he arrived, but my brothers had already disappeared. Whew, that's a relief, I thought. I don't want to scare this guy off. I like him.

I spent most of my spare time from that point on dating Jack. Jack often accompanied me to my family functions and, noticeably, Ray didn't try to molest me. I often wondered why. Was it because he had redeemed his wicked ways? Was it because Jack was around?

Even though I rarely spent time at Donna's house anymore, my stomach continued to give me trouble. Sometimes it ached, and sometimes it didn't. I just tried to ignore it and go on. In fact I didn't care because having diarrhea meant that I'd possibly lose weight and become attractive, and then someone would love me.

It didn't take very long for my relationship with Jack to become physical. At first, I resisted his advances. But he was kind and gentle and only pushed me to a point, and then he'd be very gentlemanly and back off. Jack assured me that we'd go at my pace. How different from what I was used to with Ray. I felt genuine love from Jack. Soon, I begin to treasure his touch, and my old craving for more love and affection surfaced. Often, we would lie together for hours, just holding each other. I felt comfortable and protected with Jack. I was happy with him.

Before long, however, Jack began to ask why I was "stone cold" toward him in front of other people. He said that I had ice in my veins. That's not how I felt, but I was unable to verbalize my feelings, thoughts, and emotions. I just shrugged my shoulders and gave him a cute look, hoping that would appease him. Teenage boy that he was, he couldn't resist. He would smile back at me, and all would be well again, at least for a while. Truthfully, I began to wonder about Jack's comments about my inability to even hold hands in public. Jack wanted me to display physical affection outside the bedroom, but I rarely even hugged my mom or dad. Or, should I say, my parents didn't hug me. I just didn't know how to show affection publicly. I knew Jack had a point.

Several times, I broke off our relationship. Looking back, I am not even sure why. I think I just felt too much and needed a break. Or perhaps I got scared. Jack just began accepting my "stone cold" moments. Each time, it didn't take long for us to resume our relationship. I always felt safe around Jack, and I even daydreamed about marrying him. But fate had other plans.

After high school, Jack went into military service, and I went away to college. We had a long-distance relationship for a few years, but in the end Jack ended up marrying someone else. Meanwhile, I remained emotionally undeveloped. I hadn't a clue who I was or who or what I wanted to become. So, in the great tradition of many other Americans, after college I moved out West to start my life anew. My brother, Brad, had moved to Seattle a few years earlier, and he invited me to stay with him while I established myself in the Emerald City. Amid the natural splendor of the Pacific Northwest, I decided I would begin my rocky journey of healing and self-discovery.

Part 2
Adult Life

Chapter 7:

Unraveling

Within months of moving to Seattle, I met a guy named Sam. I was desperate for love and stability in my life, and so was he. I was twenty-five, and Sam was thirty-three. We immediately began a relationship and, after a month of almost daily dates, I moved in with him. We agreed, with the naïve assuredness of new couples everywhere, that for the relationship to work there couldn't be any surprises between us. So I told Sam about Ray's inappropriate touching. Sam just shrugged his shoulders and brushed it off, saying that I had been fondled, that it happened a lot.

His reaction helped reinforce my desire to not think about it and to push any emotions about it back down inside of myself. He's right, I reasoned. After all, it wasn't like I had been raped. I had nothing to complain about, especially when compared to the horrific rape and assault victims we heard about on TV. At least, that is what I told myself.

At this stage I had stopped drinking ... totally. One morning, I woke up, decided drinking was too fattening, and that I'd rather eat chocolates for my fat calories. Sam was training for a marathon, so I joined him in healthy eating and running. Truthfully, I still hated myself so much that when Sam wasn't around, I ate junk food.

A few years later, Sam and I got married. I got pregnant, and we had a baby girl named Mandy. My new life was in full swing.

♦   ♦   ♦

"Oh, where is the stomach relief herbal stuff," I said to myself, like an addict needing a fix, searching through my purse. Mandy was young and didn't have a clue why her mommy was mumbling to herself. "I just need something to take this stomach pain away," I continued. The flight attendant stopped at my seat to see if she could be of assistance.

"No, no, I'm fine. Thank you, anyway," I said. My stomach ailments had progressed to the point that I had seen a doctor about the problem. The doctor told me I would develop an ulcer the way I was going and that I'd better learn to de-stress myself, and he gave me some pills. I had long ago used up the prescription and began to rely on herbal remedies. Going back to a doctor was out of the question because that would mean confronting the deeper reasons for my stomach pain. There was no way I was going to open Pandora's box.

I couldn't tell the doctor, or anyone, that I was afraid to take my daughter on yearly visits to Dearborn. I couldn't tell them that I watched Mandy all the time during family dinners with Ray. Life seemed ever so cruel: I had to protect Mandy but hide the truth about Ray.

I continued to fake it in front of my family; I even dutifully gave Ray a weak hug as a greeting in front of others. I stuck like glue around Mandy; since she was so young, it was easy to do. Take it year by year, I thought. I'll come up with another solution when the time comes.

Not much changed during my visits; during family barbecues I would occasionally hang around Ray while he was cooking the hamburgers and hot dogs. Often we'd be by ourselves, and it didn't take long for him to start telling me dirty jokes. I'd laugh at every one of them, out of duty more than anything. I wanted to keep a good connection with Donna.

Each time I returned to the West Coast, I'd trash myself for weeks for moving away from Michigan and settling so far away from my family. I missed Donna so much. She was still my maternal figure. Eventually, though, I just could not stand being around Ray and listening to his vulgar jokes. That, of course, made it harder to spend time with Donna.

In addition, my relationship with Sam had been rocky from the start. It just wasn't a mature partnership. We'd both brought baggage into the marriage. I had sudden rages and little patience, and he had issues with alcohol and a general lack of maturity. Sam told me to just enjoy life and be happy with what we had. A noble philosophy in theory, sure. But I knew that reality was a little more complicated than that, especially with a new little daughter to care for. Sam often asked me, "Can't you ever be happy?" It was a question that came to haunt me.

When Mandy was two years old, I entered therapy. I remember the first day I walked into the therapist's office. My opening line was, "I don't like myself." (Music to any therapist's ears, no doubt.)

First, we decided, I needed to address my bubbling rages by unraveling my childhood and, more specifically, my relationship with my mom. I couldn't believe what I learned: I was repeating my mother's rages. I made it my goal to break the cycle and not pass this terrible raging behavior on to Mandy.

As I healed myself through counseling, Sam and I grew farther and farther apart. I already had made mental preparations to divorce Sam when he informed me that he had a gender identity disorder. He wanted to have a sex-change operation; he wanted to become a woman. (To learn that story, you will need to read my second book.) In the end, counseling helped me tremendously to make the changes I needed to become a happier person and a better mom; sadly, Sam and I divorced after almost ten years of marriage.

◆   ◆   ◆

"I'm getting married again!" I screamed over the phone to Donna. "And I want you to be my maid of honor."

A few years after my divorce from Sam, I met John. He was many things Sam was not—solid, mature, emotionally and financially stable, and, thank God, thoroughly at home with his sexuality. After a year of dating, we decided to marry.

This time, I really looked forward to the fun of a wedding to plan, dresses to buy, a ring to pick out. Mandy, then eleven, and I enjoyed going to the mall together to shop for junior bridesmaid dresses. My discovery that junior bridesmaid dresses don't exactly come cheap dampened my joy but only for a moment. After all, the wedding in which Mandy would participate would be mine—no, it would be ours. And Donna would be my matron of honor. Life was grand.

During my courtship with John, I told him about Ray. He was only the second person, except for counselors, who I had ever told. Sam had been pretty dismissive of the whole thing, and I continued to toe a similar line. I insisted to John that I wanted that part of my life to remain a secret. "John, if you ever tell anyone," I warned him, "it will be a deal breaker, and I'll leave you. This is something that is extremely private to me." John didn't say much, other than to reassure me that he wasn't going to blab about it to his friends. "Bon, most guys don't talk a lot about their personal relationships. And they talk about the personal relationships of their wives even less. Don't worry, your secret's safe with me."

Finally the wedding weekend arrived. My family flew in from Detroit, and I headed off to meet them at a local hotel. It was a nice spring day, but my palms were sweating. "Gee, Bonnie, calm down. It's only your family you're meeting," I mumbled to myself. For some reason, I was excited and nervous at the same time. One, two, three, breathe deeply, my inner voice reminded me. I kept telling myself to let all of that old stuff go and just enjoy the fleeting moments of my wedding.

Most of the family had arrived a few days before the wedding and were staying at a nearby hotel. Because of work commitments, Ray would not arrive until the night before. Good, it's not Ray this time, soothed my inner voice. But once I saw Donna, I realized that old wounds can be easily exposed, even when everyone is on his or her best behavior. I realized that my secrets could slip out, so I began to eat cake. At every opportunity, and there are a lot when you're the bride, I stuffed my mouth with cake so I'd be too busy to talk and then the sugar would make me sleepy. It was my plan for ensuring a happy wedding weekend and entertaining the family.

The night before the wedding, there was another family gathering. Ray was there. John, Mandy, and I drove to the hotel to meet everyone for dinner. When it was time for me to greet Ray in front of all the relatives, my stomach churned at the thought, and I felt sweat breaking out under my arms. I saw him across the room, braced myself, and walked over. We gave each other one of those super-polite hugs, with an absolute minimum of contact. While I was leaning in, I offered my cheek, and Ray pecked it. All was well in everyone's eyes. It was disgusting for me to have to acknowledge him at all and especially to have to go through with the phony sisterly act. This was the first time that I was conscious of how wrong it felt to be so deceitful in front of my family. What bothered me most was the fact that the deceit was entirely for Ray's benefit. He was the person whose guilt I was covering. And yet I was the one with all the bad feelings. I doubt Ray even felt a twinge of guilt.

But I carried off my little act, and no one was the wiser. Gee, I should have been an actor, I thought. Next up, an academy nomination, for I'm the great pretender. Step out of the way, Meryl Streep!

The night of my wedding, I ate three pieces of cake, one from each layer. I had a fantastic time.

Ray sat at the wedding table with John and me, right next to Donna. Today, I want to puke when I think about it.

◆　◆　◆

"John, we need to talk," I said through my tears. "We're not going to make it. Hand me a tissue, I'm going to cry." "What do you mean?" he asked. Through my welled-up, teary eyes, I squeakily told him, "I've been in this place before in a marriage, and we won't make it without some counseling." He listened and said in a sturdy voice, "It's only been a few months of marriage, maybe we should give it some time." Drip, drip; tears landed on my cheeks. "No, I know, we need counseling." He gently wiped my tears away. "Okay, let's look up our insurance benefits and see what they'll pay for," he said.

Marriage at mid-life isn't necessarily easy. It was our first time in a relationship that had some maturity and thoughtfulness in it. Despite our best efforts, in those early days we clashed often. We had difficult parenting challenges with Mandy to deal with, and we fundamentally disagreed on how to approach them. Much to my surprise, when I told John we needed therapy, he didn't hesitate and found us a marriage counselor through a program at his work. The program paid for a set number of counseling visits each year, and so we began weekly therapy. "I'm feeling trapped," I told the therapist in the first session. "My childhood demons are coming back to life. How do I trust this new guy with my daughter?" Rationally, I trusted John 99.999 percent; it was just that .001 percent that was giving me trouble. John neither wanted children nor had any from past relationships. That simplified our relationship a lot, but it also made me worry that he didn't have the experience to make good judgments where Mandy was concerned. I must have had a certain level of trust in him; otherwise I wouldn't have invited him in to Mandy's and my lives. I babbled on and on to the therapist. I've noticed over the years that when an emotional fear seeps up from my past, I tend to babble and cry. John discovered early on that one of his roles was to have a tissue handy for me.

The agreement at that initial session was that once a week John would watch Mandy while I ran errands outside of the house. We also decided on a range of behaviors that were acceptable and not acceptable in front of Mandy. Eek, I thought, my stomach rebelling at the very thought of letting go and trusting. Geez, what did I get myself into? I tried to release my fear into the universe and just let it go (a technique I had learned in church).

It was, and is, so challenging not to let the scars from my past inhibit Mandy's life. But I had to try.

I decided to take a class to get me out of the house. As I walked out the door, leaving Mandy with John that first time, I asked my dad—via the spirit world; he'd passed away several years after I had moved to Seattle—to watch over her while I was gone. What else could I do? Still, the first few times John watched her, I drove home like a mad woman after class. Mandy was okay every time. Eventually, I began to relax and trust John. It was such freedom from within.

One afternoon I was sitting at the local park with one of my girlfriends and our kids. She asked me, "How do we know our kids walk to school or attend a school dance unharmed? What goes on that we don't hear about?"

"Yeah, I know it's scary," I replied. "But what kind of kids would we raise if we were by their sides twenty-four/seven?" How could we really protect our kids 100 percent? Neither one of us had the answer; instead, we let the thought linger in the air.

Now when I see an over-protective mother in the playground, I don't judge her like I might have done before I had my child. I just smile in sympathy and wonder what kind of a childhood she had.

My therapy sessions with John were successful; we'd often head into them at loggerheads, usually concerning how to deal with Mandy's difficult behavior. But we almost always left with optimism and a plan to resolve our conflicts. John's commitment to finding solutions to our issues helped deepen my trust in him and lifted my spirits immeasurably. At that point, I couldn't have asked for much more.

Chapter 8:
Telling Donna

When Mandy was in high school, I watched her body grow and develop into that of a woman's, which opened a floodgate of suppressed emotions leftover from my past. As I watched her flaunt her newfound charms with a childish innocence and confidence that belied a total ignorance of the world, I became terrified about what could happen to her. Before long, I found myself back on the same old pendulum: swinging between eating loads of candy and exercising like crazy to compensate for it. I'd have episodes in which I felt like a rat running on a wheel in a cage, desperately going nowhere but still driven toward something. For example, I once bought an old dresser from a garage sale on a Saturday morning and then was at the doctor's office on Monday with painful tetanus in my arms caused by sanding the piece all weekend. In my mind I had to refinish the dresser by the end of the weekend. I was forcing myself to perform intense physical tasks that would tire out my body, so I wouldn't have to confront my worst memories. But it didn't stop the unwanted feelings from emerging once the lights went out.

My interactions with Donna became less frequent, in part because of distance but also because I was beginning to question her opinions on many subjects. I discovered that my views on a number of fundamental religious and political issues contrasted dramatically with hers. I was a Democrat, and Donna was a Republican. At first I found this rather shocking, because Donna had been such a guiding light to us kids during our formative years, at a time when no one else was providing guidance. But as my confidence grew, my thoughts were liberated. I realized that I could have my own well-reasoned opinions and even challenge hers.

To be honest, I could challenge her opinions only internally. I was still a long way from openly confronting Donna on various topics.

In 2004, Mandy and I delayed our summer visit to Dearborn so that I could attend my twenty-fifth class reunion in October. That was the class reunion where I met Jack and revealed my great secret. I called Donna to find out why she and Ray had separated. After all, I'd shared all the details of my embarrassing divorce with her. One thing I had heard was that Ray had told a highly classified secret to their kids. "Donna, what secret did Ray tell your kids that you can't forgive him for?" I inquired with a gulp. But Donna wasn't willing to share the reason for the breakup with anyone. Please, oh, please tell me it's not about my secret, I thought. My imagination was working overtime, trying to figure out what was behind her decision. Had Ray had an affair? Did he finally get caught with an underage girl? Could it be that I was not the only one? I puzzled over the mystery. It was a big, big, big secret because Donna's kids had stopped talking to her. But Donna was determined; she wouldn't reveal the secret to anyone.

She told me they that they had simply grown apart, but I didn't buy it. To this day, she won't discuss her marriage and what led to the separation. To this day, I don't know the secret. I've come to think that Donna is a better keeper of secrets than I was.

While I was in Dearborn, we planned to spend an afternoon together. Donna, Mandy, and I went shopping for clothes at Fairlane Town Center, one of my old stomping grounds. We were filling time as we waited for the next Ford truck factory tour at the automaker's historic River Rouge plant. We were back in Ford country, after all.

Mandy was in the dressing room in one of the mall's shops, and Donna and I sat waiting, alone among the clothes racks. Donna looked both stressed and despondent, though I knew that she was trying to hold things together so that Mandy and I would enjoy our visit. For some reason, almost without realizing it, I began firing questions at her. "So, Donna," I asked, "what's the thing with Ray? Did he have an affair?"

She told me that she knew of no affairs, and she wasn't about to employ a private investigator to find out. All of a sudden, I could feel my entire body language and facial expression changing. It was as if the need to tell Donna the truth about Ray had become a physical force, completely overwhelming my reluctance to blurt it out. Donna read it on my face.

"You know something," she said.

I looked away.

"Come on, tell me," she coaxed, but with a wary expression that revealed that she really didn't want to hear what I had to tell her.

I had no conscious thought about whether or how the words would come out. It was as if my mouth, detached from my brain, began working on its own. I simply said, "It was me."

Oh, my god! I had just revealed the biggest, deepest, darkest secret of my life to the person on whom it would have the greatest impact, after me. But once I began the story, I wasn't about to stop. And I was remarkably calm.

"What do you mean?" asked Donna.

"Ray was all over me, starting when I was twelve years old."

"What?" she asked. "What?" But she'd heard me. She began pacing the floor of the store. Detached and unemotional, I explained what had happened all those years before. Once the dam was broken, the words poured out. "He molested a young girl while you were busy making house," I told her. "And that girl was me."

Finally, I realized that I'd said too much and stopped blabbing. All was quiet for a long moment. Donna told me that she had been praying hard that very morning for a sign that would tell her whether or not to continue the marriage. Sadly, her prayers had been answered.

I looked at her and shrugged my shoulders. The answer couldn't have been more obvious. I didn't feel at all upset that I'd finally blurted out the truth. In my opinion, destiny had brought us here and caused us to have this long-overdue conversation. It was a sad time, but I didn't yet feel its full impact. I was numb but filled with a surprising confidence too, that I had done the right thing by telling my sister.

Mandy returned, and for once I was thankful that she took forever to choose her clothes. Somehow, Donna suppressed her shock. We purchased the clothes and—it seems ridiculous now—went on the Ford tour. Both Donna and I were in such a traumatized state that we were unable to even think about changing our schedule. I doubt that the tour guide ever had two less attentive women in tow. As we stared at the machinery, I began to feel bad for Donna. I could imagine how hard it must be for her, struggling to appear relaxed and normal in front of us while replaying the early years of her marriage over and over in her head. I began to feel guilty. Bad Bonnie, how could you tell her in such a casual way? Bad Bonnie, you should have waited and told her at a better time. The thoughts tumbled around in my head. I had trouble meeting her gaze.

And you know what? I can't tell you one thing about that truck factory.

Everything was a blur, but we somehow made it back to Mom's house. Donna dropped us off, and we waved good-bye as she drove away. At one point on the drive back, Donna turned to me and asked, "Bonnie, what do you need?" I wasn't quite sure what she meant. Was she offering to pay for counseling? Was she asking if I needed a shoulder to cry on? I couldn't tell. I thought to myself, Oh, Donna, you're not responsible, Ray is; Ray should be asking me this. I looked at her and said that I was fine. It wasn't true, of course. I had now divulged my great secret to a member of my family. I shivered at the thought. It was just a matter of time before it spread to the rest of the clan.

Later, I lay in my old bed, in my old bedroom; Mandy was on the floor in a sleeping bag. I searched for some chocolate candies I had stashed in my bedroom when I arrived in town. And, ahh, I found them. Comfort.

I didn't tell anyone else my secret during that trip. I knew that Donna needed time to process what I had said. I figured she'd tell the rest of the family when she was ready.

Chapter 9:

Letting Go

"Um, yes, I'd like to make an appointment … about some childhood stuff." I stuttered into the new therapist's answering machine, then left my phone number for a callback. After I told Donna about Ray, it was back to therapy for me, this time, on my own.

In the therapist's office for the first time, I sat down on the couch and stared out the window. "Yes, right. Here we go," I began. "I was inappropriately touched by my brother-in-law, Ray, for a number of years, starting when I was a kid. But it was minor stuff so I figure my therapy should only need to last about three months or less."

I looked at her, waiting to see if she agreed. She considered what I'd said. "How about we take it one step at a time," she said.

Shit! I felt doomed. I wanted help, and yet I didn't. I just wanted it all to go away. "Okay, fine," I said.

I had been to several therapists by this point and I was getting used to relaying my life's story. I inhaled a deep breath and began babbling.

"Let's see: Donna divorced Ray after I told her about what he'd done to me. That was well over a year ago. The following summer, during my annual visit, Donna avoided me. She told me her feelings were 'too raw.' I felt hurt but tried to understand. We agreed to write each other. Her first letter asked why I hadn't told her about it when it actually happened. I replied that there was too much shame, but that was an answer that I'd taken from a text book. Actually, I'd really like to know why I didn't say anything to Donna during all that time. Maybe you can shed some light on that?

"Anyway, it started during my trip to Detroit for the reunion, when I told my old boyfriend and Donna. Then a year later during my next visit, you know, when Donna would no longer see me, I almost told my older brother and his wife. But I held back. I don't know why. I'd like to know that too. Why is it so hard to tell anyone? I keep telling myself that I need to give Donna time to adjust. Well, at least that's what I've been telling myself up to now.

"During all of these trips to Dearborn, I've never told my mom. Now I'm going to take another trip back there, and I have a couple of problems. For one, Donna and I are no longer communicating at all. Our letter writing only lasted for a few letters. I want to go to Detroit and visit without contacting her, but my brother Brad, with whom I will stay, doesn't want to be caught in the middle of anything complicated. He tells me that if he has a barbecue at his house, he'll invite everyone. So, should I just tell everyone?

"Oh, but I can't tell my mom yet. She's in poor health and doesn't need this kind of drama. Oh, yeah, one more thing, I am having a hard time with crying these days. It seems that out of the blue, I just cry. That isn't like me. I usually can fake happiness in front of others."

I took a breath. "That about covers it," I said with a sheepish smile. Whew. Then I sat there, smiling at my new therapist, hoping she wouldn't ask too many probing questions.

At our next session, I walked in upset and teary. I wondered what she was thinking. "It's time to tell my brothers and sisters," I said. "The issue is, as I told you before, with my brother Brad. I'd like to stay at his house, but I've asked him to not let Donna know. Brad says he isn't going to play that game. I understand his desire to not get into complicated issues between his sisters. And

Brad doesn't know the source of the tension between us. I feel the universe is telling me it's time to share my story about Ray with Brad." My therapist nodded understandingly, and said that she understood how emotional this was. Sitting on the couch, I finally thought, for heaven's sakes, what's the big deal? It's not like I'm the queen of England. What do I care if others know?

Yet, just talking to her about it made me extremely nervous. Without even realizing it, I'd grabbed a pillow from the couch and was tightly squeezing it to my stomach. I couldn't jog enough miles, swim enough laps, or dance enough Jazzercise to relax the tension I had inside. She and I talked through several scenarios that could occur in Detroit, discussing how to deal with each of them. "I really should have prepared myself better before telling Donna," I said to the therapist. Oh well, I'll kick myself later about that, I thought to myself.

Later that night, as I sat blindly watching television, I had an idea: I'd tell Brad over the phone. I hadn't thought of that before. I thought I had to tell everyone in person. But telling him over the phone would solve a couple of problems. First, he'd understand the tension between me and Donna, and he'd be more willing to let me stay there without telling her. I wouldn't have to wait any longer. And it might even be easier to say everything over the phone.

Here I go, I thought, opening Pandora's box again.

"Hello, Brad, it's me," I said, when he picked up the phone. "Listen, I need to speak to you and Tara at the same time." I waited while Brad got Tara, whom he married years ago, when he was just out of college.

The seconds stretched out. My stomach was in knots. Why do I do this to myself, I thought.

Brad and Tara got on the line. I started. "Well, I'm going to tell you something, and I'll probably cry through it. You see, I was sexually molested when we were growing up."

Silence.

"It was someone in our family." I grabbed a tissue and tried to control my voice. "Can you guess who it was?"

It was a stupid thing to ask because neither Brad nor Tara was going to start tossing out names in response. But my mind was buzzing, my stomach was turning flips, and my hands were shaking.

"No guess, huh? Okay, I'll tell you. It was Ray."

More silence.

"It started when I was twelve." I went on to describe what had happened in broad brushstrokes, leaving out the sensitive details.

Brad and Tara had little to say in response; they mostly mumbled expressions of surprise and dismay. When we were done, I hung up the phone, my hands trembling. Now what, I wondered. How will this change my relations with the family? I guess I'll find out.

Later that summer, I arrived at Brad and Tara's house. I was alone, without Mandy or John, for this family visit. I had wondered what kind of reception I would receive, so I was happy and relieved when I received a big hug from each of them. I really needed that reassuring gesture of love. Then it was down to business. I knew that it was also time to tell my younger brother Tom, who lived in the area. The twist was that Tom worked for Ray, who had owned a company with Donna until the divorce ended her involvement.

Brad and I went to Tom's house; his two young girls were taking their afternoon nap. Sitting across from Tom and his wife, I suddenly felt twelve years old again and at a loss for words. Breathing in deeply, I encouraged myself to be calm, to act like an adult. What is this, I thought; my heart is beginning to beat faster. Calm down, Bonnie. Okay, just tell them. And I did.

After I was finished, I thought with relief, Wow, I did it! I was able to say it like an adult and look them in the eyes at the same time. I asked if they'd had any idea who it was. No, they both said; neither of them had any idea. I couldn't help but wonder if they simply didn't want to name someone and have it turn out to be someone else.

"Ahh, all right. It was Ray." Tom was visibly agitated. "Why didn't you tell me sooner?" he asked. This is such a common question, which revealed that he, like most people, seemed to have a general misunderstanding of how difficult it is to be a victim. As if telling anyone such a thing is easy.

"Now the last two years at work make sense," Tom continued. It seems that Ray had given Tom some of the least popular work assignments and was generally treating him badly.

"I'm sorry," was all I could think of to say. Geez, why am I the one apologizing, I thought. I began to question why was I even telling my family at all. Was it to warn them because they had young children? Was it because I wanted validation and sympathy? Or did I have a need to explain my chaotic life and my sometimes goofy demeanor? The answer was a mystery to me. Um, this would be a good therapy discussion, I noted to myself. Good, I'll get my money's worth. I smiled at Tom and his wife. "It's over and I'm okay," I said.

Later I heard through the family grapevine that Tom was very angry when he heard my news and had felt like physically assaulting Ray. But obviously he wouldn't—and financially couldn't—since Ray had deep pockets and could and would have sued him for all he was worth. At least, it was nice to know that my brother wanted to stand up for me.

Before I flew home, I stopped by to say hello to Mom. She and I had had a past falling out over Mandy, so we were not on comfortable terms. I chose not to tell her about Ray. Instead, we talked about the weather.

Back in Seattle, I told my therapist the details of the visit. One of the things that still haunts me is why I didn't tell anyone sooner. I knew that books on this subject and all the professionals I had ever heard always stress how difficult it is for the victim to speak up. And yet, somehow that answer wasn't enough for me. I should have been different.

The session ended, and we promised to pick up the discussion at that point the next time. But a few days later I called and cancelled my appointments with her. I said that I didn't have the money and that Mandy needed me. That was just an excuse. The layers of my life, like an onion, were peeling back. I just wanted to freeze time and stop crying for awhile.

Chapter 10:

Flood Gates

Another year passed, and once again it was time to plan my annual summer visit to Dearborn. I experienced my usual seesaw of emotions. What was it about my visits to Dearborn? One minute cold nerves gripped my stomach, and the next minute I was filled with anticipation and excitement to see my family. Karen and I made plans to fly to Dearborn at the same time so we could help Mom put her house up for sale. At the age of eighty-one, Mom had reached a stage in her life where she needed to move into senior housing.

Karen hadn't been to Dearborn for more than ten years. She had followed her husband to Texas and then Colorado Springs, enthusiastically joining the huge conservative Christian enclave there. Many of my brothers and sisters were excited to visit with her, but not Donna. The feud between the two oldest sisters went way back to childhood—over what, exactly, was never clear to me. But the blood between them was bad. Donna actually said that she didn't want Karen to attend her funeral when the time came. But I got along well with Karen, perhaps because we'd both experienced major marital and financial problems. We were also both used to being called "the out-of-towners" within the family circle. Although the phrase may sound benign, in fact, it had an edge to it. For years, some of my family had felt that since Karen and I had left the area, we no longer had standing when it came to making decisions about our parents and their needs.

Karen and I walked into Mom's house, and there she was, sitting in her recliner. She was hunched over her knitting, with a shawl wrapped around her shoulders. As I gazed at her wrinkled face and hands, I realized immediately that the past hurts between us no longer mattered. It was time for me to put my grievances aside and do all I could to maximize her comfort in her old age.

After Karen and I settled in, we all sat together in the cozy living room along with our brother Joe, whose bouts with drugs and alcohol and a major car accident had rendered him disabled. We were talking about the family, about who was mad at whom and why, when my mind began to wander. I had decided that it was time for me to complete the circle and tell the rest of the family about Ray. I decided to wait for an appropriate opening in the conversation. But it didn't take long for my inside volcano to erupt, and I blurted it out.

"I want to tell you all something," I said. "Ray sexually abused me when I was a child." There was a startled pause. Even today, I am amazed at the different types of reactions from people. Karen, with sadness in her eyes, came to my side. Joe was taken back, and my mom said simply, "Well, thank goodness you weren't raped."

Then, much to my surprise, the conversation turned into a discussion about others Ray had or might have "touched." Karen told us that one time, when she was visiting home during a college break, Ray aggressively cornered her and began trying to kiss her and such. Luckily, she was able to push him off her. There was no telling what would have happened if she hadn't had the physical strength to defend herself.

I was dumbstruck. All this time, I had been carrying this huge secret and Karen had been doing the same thing. I remembered that my therapist had told me, "You're probably not the only one"; her prediction had come true. No sooner did this thought go through my mind than Joe piped up. "Well, there is something I heard through the rumor mill. Someone told me years ago about our cousin/sister, Joanne."

Our eyes wide, Karen and I stared at each other. "Oh, my god, not Joanne," one of us said. Inside, I could feel my outrage at Ray doing battle with sadness for my cousin. We had no way to confirm Joe's story that Ray had molested Joanne. She had died several years earlier, and we had lost contact with Dave. It would have to remain a rumor. Now it was my turn to "have no idea this had happened." My God, this is becoming surreal, I thought. Karen and I went into the kitchen and prepared dinner, puzzling and speculating at the new information we had to digest.

The next day Karen and I began cleaning and sorting through things to get our mother's house ready for its sale. There was plenty of work to do, since our family had lived there for some sixty years. We couldn't stop talking about Ray and the extent to which he had messed up our family.

We took a break in the afternoon to meet another family member for lunch. After telling her all that we knew and had learned, Karen and I both saw an acknowledgement in her face. No, it can't be, I thought. She had had an incident with Ray as well? This was unbelievable. The three of us sat in stunned amazement. What a vile man, I thought. It was like a sickness with him. I never would have believed that Ray had been so extravagant in his behavior. And none of this would have come to light if I had not spoken up.

The flood gates had finally split wide open. It was clear that Ray had made aggressive and persistent sexual advances to several family members, including kids as young as twelve, like me, and maybe even younger, like Joanne. And here he had played the wonderful husband to Donna all these years, living a comfortable lifestyle, and presiding as the owner of a hugely profitable family company.

On the flight back to Seattle after that trip, I simply could not believe what I had learned. There were five women in my family circle, and apparently Ray made sexual advance to three of the them. And yet it had taken thirty years for all of us to piece it together. Each of us had kept the humiliating truth to ourselves for a whole host of reasons, but in doing so we had enabled Ray to the point where he felt free to molest females at will. A man who should have been behind bars or in a psychiatric ward had instead played the role of respected husband and head of the family, all the while preying on its women and children.

Epilogue

I've thought a lot about all of the damage that happened to me over the years. I've come to several conclusions, hopefully ones I can use to move forward with my life.

Mom

I discovered she had a number of health issues, including chronic neurological disorder, epilepsy, mood disorder, and erythropoietic protoporphyria (EEP), a rare genetic disease.

Because of her epilepsy, as a girl she had been locked in closets, whipped, and subjected to many other brutal forms of "discipline." Most important, during her childhood, she never received any established epilepsy medicine. She told me that her parents didn't have the money. Instead, my mother turned to the Catholic Church, hoping that if she were devout God would deliver her from her affliction. She intensely believed God would have mercy on her soul and give her a miracle, namely, cure her of epilepsy.

Later when she was married, every time she was pregnant (which was often, being Catholic and all), she was advised to go off her epilepsy medicine. After she was done nursing the infant (for three days), she would resume taking the medicine. But by then, she was usually pregnant again. No wonder she was an emotional volcano. Not long ago, she told me, "I was always pregnant because in between you kids, I had miscarriages." When I was a child, Mom's epilepsy medicine was upgraded to more modern drugs. Although they were generally more effective, the process of switching between them "was awful," she said. "I felt so doped up all that time."

When my mom was in her eighties, I asked her how many children she had wanted to have. "None," she admitted. "But I didn't have a choice, I was Catholic." I wasn't upset with her honest answer. In her day, the way she was raised, having no children simply was not an option—certainly, not if you were going to be married.

Clearly, occasionally whacking us with a spoon wasn't the worst of it. Far more damaging was her mood disorder, which caused her emotional blackmail and other manipulations. We were never encouraged to speak honestly or to be open about our feelings. In fact, we learned to hide them as a survival technique. We had no training in analyzing our emotions and inner thoughts and no experience in sharing them because our parents didn't show us how. My mother's random jealously, paranoia, and extreme mood swings created a lot of chaos in the household. So we blindly felt our way through childhood without insight and understanding and without that essential emotional safe harbor.

For all the fun I had, my childhood memories are clouded with embarrassment and pain. I was constantly confused about how members of the family behaved and how I felt about it. I loved my mom like any child does and craved her attention and approval. It rarely came. And yet, I couldn't stop myself from wanting to make her happy. I'd listen with eagerness to her stories, hoping to please her.

But then the bad days would return. There was no rhyme or reason behind her sudden rages, and she would lose herself in them.

Perhaps a small part of it was generational; the rebellious 1960s did not yet have a presence in our neighborhood, and questioning the Greatest Generation, the men and women who survived the Great Depression and won the war for freedom and democracy, was tantamount to sacrilege.

In my mom's mind, she was a better parent to her kids than her mother had been to her. She encouraged education, history, traveling, and adventure. Physically, we were well taken care of, without a doubt. However, emotionally, we were crippled by her volcanic rages. I often wonder why no one stopped her rages. Why did my dad put up with that behavior in his household?

To top all this off, we learned that my mom has EPP, which makes her photosensitive to the sun. This painful disease wasn't even known to medical science until 1960. It usually flares up during the spring and summer months. My mother had to wear long-sleeve shirts, gloves, and hats or stay indoors. No wonder she felt left out and got jealous when I was outside with my dad.

Today, Mom is old and frail. She has moved out to the Pacific Northwest, near my house in Seattle, and I am her family caregiver. It is an odd feeling to be in charge of her day-to-day life. In her moments of uncertainly and insecurity, I often hear her voice her secret fears. Once, I called her from work to check on her. She was having difficulty with the transition from her life-long home to a brand new city and living space. I innocently suggested that maybe we should look for another place in the area. Later that afternoon, I stopped by after work to see how she was doing. When I walked in, she was sitting in her rocking chair with the rosary in her hand. Clearly frightened, she looked up and asked if I was moving her to an institution. She looked like she was thirteen years old. I realized that one of her childhood fears had been that she would be institutionalized when her epilepsy surfaced. I learned a lot about her at that moment. Her past fears are intense inside of her. I am sure I'll learn more about my mom as I continue on this journey with her.

She is taking a new drug for her epilepsy, which is far easier on her body and soothes her emotions. Her doctor told her that the first change would be that she'd feel as if a fog had lifted from around her head. Even her sense of smell would improve. I sat there in the room, delighted for her, and also ruing the fact that this drug had not been available during my childhood … or hers.

It is time for me to let go of the sadness and anger. Instead, I'll continue to enjoy her company and her sense of humor.

Donna

Donna no longer talks to Karen or to me, which means that Donna's grown children don't talk to me either. She has never said why; instead, she just cut me off. The supposed reason had to do with me moving Mom from Dearborn into a senior living facility in Seattle so that I could take care of her on a daily basis. This responsibility meant that I would oversee Mom's finances. The situation got ugly when Donna accused me of trying to steal money from our mom. News flash, I thought. Mom is not rich, and everyone in the family knows that. So why would Donna say that about me?

It is interesting that Donna had said the same thing about Karen for over twenty-five years. Whenever our family would talk about Karen, Donna would suggest that our older sister was positioning herself to inherit Mom's money. Everyone at the table would sit there quietly when she'd say this. Donna was the leader, and her word was usually final. Now Donna was using the same line against me. Was it because I had stood up to her about how to care for Mom?

Donna had been in charge for so many years. But now we were older, and we all had ideas about how to proceed. Once again, our family had never been the type to openly discuss and resolve problems, learning to give and take, win and lose, while maintaining our love for one another, regardless. In fact, one female family member still doesn't want to tell Donna about her ugly run-in with Ray. She told me the reason is because she doesn't want to ruin her relationship with Donna.

But what about exposing Ray? Isn't that the important point? Shouldn't the females in the family unite, get all the secrets out, and help protect ourselves and our kids? But I understand the thought pattern. It took me years to wake up and realize that protecting Donna was a dysfunctional way to live. As a result, I imagine that Donna and I will never speak again. Now that I've broken free from the unquestioning hold she had over us, I doubt we'll be able to restore our relationship. The reason is simple: I've grown up. She will only accept the relationship under the old power structure, and I can no longer accept that. I may have won the Golden Globe award for acting and pretending over the years that all was well, but Donna wins the Oscar for being the greatest keeper of secrets.

Ray

Do I want to meet Ray face to face and say my piece? No. Do I want to write Ray a letter instead? No. If I were around Ray, I'm afraid that I'd revert to that twelve-year-old: goofy, unable to clearly state my feelings, flustered, and angry. It wouldn't be a therapeutic experience for me. At times I get pissed off that Ray lives a life of wealth. He made money hand over fist with the business he inherited from his father, the one that Donna was a part of for years. He owns private planes, expensive cars, land, and tailored suits. I have no idea if he has any remorse about his predatory, destructive, and awesomely selfish behavior. It boils down to this: I'd have Ray wear a scarlet letter "M" for "molester" on his forehead for ten years. It is time for him to feel shame for his sick, selfish, destructive behavior.

My life

I have struggled for many years to rid my life of financial and emotional chaos. I've been in and out of therapy since I arrived in Seattle in the 1980s. As of this writing, I'm back in therapy. This time I joined an all-female group with an eight-month commitment. This style of therapy includes more than talking; we have foam balls, squares, and bats that we use to physically release some of our inner volcanoes.

During my first, disastrous marriage, I went into a deep depression. I had been an athlete all my life, but it became that I could hardly walk. The smallest noise would hurt my head so badly that even the touch of man's caressing hand on my head felt like a bomb exploding inside me. And, most important, I had a difficult time processing words. Someone would say something to me, and I'd look like a deer caught in headlights. It would take all my concentration just to understand the words. I finally sought medical help. That resulted in a course of antidepressants. The antidepressants, therapy, and my desire to bring joy into my soul were the cures I needed.

Today, I'm much more in control of my inner volcano because when I feel the lava bubbling inside, I pause, take note of which wound is coming to surface, and move to release it. Best of all, through all these years, I've worked hard to become a better parent. I'm proud of Mandy. She has been at the receiving end of some of my rages and the chaos caused by marriage number one. She has her own journey to take now.

Today, I have peace and happiness in my life. I feel released from much of my inner turmoil. I still can hardly believe that three females in my family were violated by Ray, by one degree or another, and yet it took over thirty years to share our common experiences. We had endless opportunities together, and yet we never shared our secret.

My wish is to enlighten other women through my story; maybe it will help others in some way to free themselves, even a little, from their own turmoil. Maybe someone else will find the courage to set her secret free.

Suggested Group Discussion

1. Why was Bonnie so passive when she was being molested? Why didn't she tell her parents or either of her sisters?

2. What signals did the adults miss? What might have warned them that things were not right between Ray and Bonnie?

3. Do you think Ray felt any guilt about what he did?

4. Discuss the different responses from others when Bonnie told her secret to family and friends. How would you respond in a similar situation? What did Bonnie want to hear from them? What did she need to hear?